D1602240

Shortcut to Norwegian:
Beginner's Guide to Quickly Learning the Basics of the Norwegian Language

INGE STENBERG

CONTENTS

Introduction: How to Learn Norwegian   1

The Norwegian Alphabet   5

Norwegian Pronunciation Guide   7

Norwegian – English Cognates   11

Noun Genders and Plurals   15

Common Norwegian Nouns   19

Pronouns   21

Norwegian Verbs: Present and Past Tenses   25

Common Norwegian Verbs   29

Adjectives   31

Norwegian Numbers, Days and Months   33

Useful Norwegian Phrases   35

Glossary –Thematic Order   37

Glossary –Alphabetical Order   43

INTRODUCTION:
HOW TO LEARN NORWEGIAN

SETTING GOALS

Learning a new language is seen by many, especially English speakers, as an extremely complicated, time-consuming task and one that above a certain age is not really practical, or even possible, anymore. Learning a new language can indeed be a lot of work, but it is nowhere near impossible; in fact in many societies around the world it is the norm to speak more than one language, and sometimes several. As an English speaker you probably don't feel that you need to speak any other language and for the most part that is true. But despite this, you want to learn a new language, or are at least considering it, or you wouldn't be reading this. Learning a new language can be an extremely enriching experience and one that I feel everyone should at least honestly attempt.

What I encourage you to do is to think about what you are trying to achieve by learning Norwegian.

You will not learn to speak Norwegian so well that in a few short months you are confused for a Norwegian native speaker. In fact it is unlikely this will ever happen. Instead of thinking in those kinds of terms, think about, or better yet visualize, what you want to be able to do with the language.

Do you want to get more out of a trip to Norway? Do you want to communicate better with Norwegian family members? Do you want to make an effort to learn the native language of someone you love?

These are all very achievable goals.

I have written this book, not to teach you how to speak fluent Norwegian in one week, as that would be impossible anyways, but to give you a shortcut to the Norwegian language. This shortcut is achieved by focusing on the areas where Norwegian is similar to English and by giving you the rules of Norwegian, without getting hung up on the exceptions, so that you can start understanding and speaking Norwegian much faster than with traditional methods.

Traditional classroom methods of teaching a foreign language, like the ones you probably remember from school, can be successful with some committed students, but they can take many years to achieve results. Since what is taught in the beginning is often not very useful, if the student does not continue with the course he or she will often remember very little. In contrast to that approach this book will give you an extremely useful introduction to the Norwegian language. After completing this book it will be up to you if you continue to learn the language, but even if you go no further than this guide, the basic building blocks of the Norwegian language that you will have learned from this book will be useful in the future and bring you closer to your Norwegian language goals.

TAKE ADVANTAGE OF ONLINE TOOLS

The internet age has forever changed our approach to language learning. It is now easy, with no more than a quick Google search and a few clicks of the mouse, to listen to Norwegian radio, watch a Norwegian comedy or read the news in Norwegian. In addition to media for native speakers, there is a seemingly never-ending supply of material to learn almost any new language.

Two tools that I recommend to complement this book are:

forvo.com
A language book like this one can be a great introduction to a new language. As adults we crave explanations as to why the language works the way it does and try to find the underlying "rules" or "patterns" and books like this are useful to give these explanations. The major downside to language books of course is that you cannot hear the language spoken. Forvo solves this problem.

Go to forvo.com and type in any Norwegian word in this book and immediately hear it pronounced by a native speaker!

<u>Anki</u>
It has been said that repetition is the mother of all learning, and when it comes to learning vocabulary it is hard to argue with this logic. Anki is a spaced-repetition flashcard program that you can install on a computer or as an app on your smartphone or tablet. Make flashcards of the Norwegian words you want to memorize and Anki will decide when you need to see that word next in order to efficiently memorize it.

It is my sincere hope that this book proves useful to you and helps you achieve your Norwegian language goals.

THE NORWEGIAN ALPHABET

The Norwegian language uses the same Latin alphabet as English, but with the addition of 3 new letters after the z. The letters with their names in Norwegian are given in the table below:

Norwegian Letter	Norwegian Name
a	a
b	be
c	se
d	de
e	e
f	eff
g	ge
h	hå
i	i
j	je/jådd
k	kå
l	ell
m	em
n	enn

o	o
p	pe
q	ku
r	ærr
s	ess
t	te
u	u
v	ve
w	dåbbelt-ve
x	eks
y	y
z	sett
æ	æ
ø	ø
å	å

NORWEGIAN PRONUNCIATION GUIDE

Pronunciation is one of the more difficult aspects of the Norwegian language and the relationship between the written word and the spoken word is not always clear. Norwegian has silent letters and a few strange sounds that make it difficult to achieve correct pronunciation for an English speaker.

Below is a rough guide to reading words in Norwegian. Remember that it is common to find words that break these "rules" and spoken Norwegian does not always closely follow the written word. Moreover, the Norwegian language is made up of different dialects which influence the pronunciation of various words.

Norwegian Letter(s)	Pronunciation Guideline
a	"**a**" as in f**a**ther
b	"**b**" as in **b**eer
c	"**k**" as in **k**ite before a, o, or u; "**s**" as in **s**ea elsewhere
d	"**d**" as in **d**og; after l or n or before s or t is usually silent; it is also often silent at the end of words
e	"**ai**" as in **ai**r or "**e**" as in b**e**d
f	"**f**" as in **f**eet

g	"**g**" as in **g**ood normally; before i or y: "**y**" as in **y**es; silent when a word ends with ig
h	"**h**" as in **h**is; silent before a consonant
i	"**ee**" as in b**ee** or "**i**" as in s**i**t
j	"**y**" as in **y**es
k	"**k**" as in **k**ick normally; before i, j or y: a soft "**sh**" sound, like the **ch** in German i**ch**
l	"**l**" as in **l**ight
m	"**m**" as in **m**eat
n	"**n**" as in **n**et
o	"**oo**" as in f**oo**d or "**o**" as in c**o**t
p	"**p**" as in **p**ie
q	similar to English
r	"**r**" as in the Spanish to**r**o; Beginners can substitute an English "**r**"
rs	"**sh**" as in **sh**eep
s	always "**s**" as in **s**it; never with a "**z**" sound like in hou**s**es
sj	"**sh**" as in **sh**eep
sk	"**sh**" as in **sh**eep

skj	"**sh**" as in **sh**eep
t	"**t**" as in **t**en normally; silent when a word ends in et
u	"**u**" as in b**u**tcher
v	"**v**" as in **v**an; sometimes silent at the end of words
w	"**v**" as in **v**an
x	"**x**" as in ta**x**i
y	"**u**" as in c**u**te but with lips more rounded. Similar to the French "u" or German "ü"
z	"**s**" as in **s**et
æ	"**a**" as in b**a**d
ø	"**ir**" as in th**ir**st but shorter. Similar to the German ö
å	"**o**" as in m**o**re or "**o**" as in c**o**t

NORWEGIAN–ENGLISH COGNATES

Norwegian and English are closely related languages that share a lot of their core vocabulary. This includes:

ANIMALS

katt – cat
fisk – fish
mus – mouse
ko – cow
lam – lamb

PARTS OF THE BODY

arm – arm
finger – finger
kne – knee
fot – foot
hår – hair

HOUSEHOLD ITEMS

hus – house
rom – room
dør – door
vindu – window
kniv – knife

FAMILY MEMBERS

moder – mother (usually shortened to **mor**)
fader – father (usually shortened to **far**)
broder – brother (usually shortened to **bror**)
søster – sister
sønn – son
datter – daughter

SIMPLE VERBS

drikke – drink
kysse – kiss
fly – fly
gå – go
kan – can (be able to)

As an English speaker these cognates are very helpful and make learning the Norwegian language much easier than learning an unrelated language. Pay attention to words that are cognates but do not have the exact same meaning in English as in Norwegian. For example **hund** in Norwegian is "dog" and not just a hunting dog like the English word "hound". There are also some false-cognates (or "false-friends"), i.e. words that look similar but whose meanings are not the same. A famous example is the Norwegian word **gift**, which means either "poison" or "married" but never "gift"!

In addition to basic vocabulary, the grammar of Norwegian has a lot in common with the grammar of English.

The word order is largely the same:

Du kan drikke kaffe med melk.
You can drink coffee with milk.

Kan jeg sitte her?
Can I sit here?

There are no case declensions in Norwegian except for the genitive (possessive form), which adds an –s ending in a similar way to English.

ei jente
a girl

ei jentes hus
a girl's house (no apostrophe in Norwegian)

Norwegian and English have similar systems of "weak" verbs and "strong" verbs. Like in English, "weak" verbs add a –d or –t sound in the past tense and are considered regular, whereas "strong" verbs change vowel sounds in the past tense and are irregular. For example:

<u>Weak verb</u>
jeg kysser – jeg kysset – jeg har kysset
I kiss – I kissed – I have kissed

<u>Strong verb</u>
vi synger – vi sang – vi har sunget
we sing – we sang – we have sung

The structure of Norwegian is in many ways similar to that of English, and this is a real advantage to learning Norwegian as an English speaker.

If only the pronunciation was as similar as the grammar is!

NOUN GENDERS AND PLURALS

GENDER

Like most European languages, but unlike English, Norwegian nouns have grammatical gender. Norwegian nouns come in one of three genders: masculine, feminine or neuter. Although most nouns match their biological gender, i.e. "boy" is masculine and "girl" is feminine, the distribution of non-human nouns into genders is largely arbitrary and the gender of a noun must therefore be memorized alongside the noun.

The gender of the noun determines the articles that are used with that noun. The word for "a/an" in Norwegian changes depending on the gender of the noun, **en** for masculine nouns, **ei** for feminine nouns and **et** for neuter nouns.

en gutt – ei jente – et hus
a boy – a girl – a house

The word for "the" in Norwegian actually attaches to the end of the word and is different depending on the gender of the noun. The three forms are **–en** for masculine, **–a** for feminine and **–et** for neuter. If the word already ends in an **–e**, this **–e** is dropped before adding the ending.

gutten – jenta – huset
the boy – the girl– the house

In Norwegian, the masculine forms can be used instead of the feminine forms for feminine nouns. Whether to use the feminine or masculine forms is a choice and neither is necessarily more "correct" although using the masculine forms may seem more formal or bookish to Norwegians.

Because it is easier to remember two forms instead of three, I recommend beginners focus on using the masculine forms for both masculine and feminine nouns. Both of the following forms are correct:

ei jente OR **en jente**
a girl

jenta OR **jenten**
the girl

PLURALS

To form the plural form of nouns in Norwegian, the most common way is to add –er to masculine and feminine nouns and to make no change to neuter nouns. This means that neuter nouns are often the same in the singular and the plural (like "deer" in English). If the word already ends in –e, then the masculine and feminine plurals just add an –r to the end of the singular form.

gutter – jenter – hus
boys – girls – houses

One common exception to this rule is for words that already end in –er. These words often add an –e to the noun to form the plural form.

amerikaner – amerikanere
American – Americans

Although these rules are true for most Norwegian nouns, there are irregular nouns that do not follow any rules when forming plurals. This is similar to the situation in English with words like child – children, foot – feet, tooth – teeth etc. These nouns must therefore be memorized as there are no rules that can be learned as a shortcut. Thankfully the number of irregular nouns in Norwegian is not too large.

Like in the singular, to say "the boys", we add an ending to the word in Norwegian. This form, called the plural definite form, is – **ene** for almost all nouns. If the word already ends in –**e**, then remove the –**e** before adding –**ene**.

en gutt – gutten – gutter – guttene
a boy – the boy – boys – the boys

ei / en jente – jenta / jenten – jenter – jentene
a girl – the girl – girls – the girls

et hus – huset – hus – husene
a house – the house – houses – the houses

For words that already end in –**er**, the plural form adds –**ne** instead of –**ene**.

en amerikaner – amerikaneren – amerikanere – amerikanerne
an American – the American – Americans – the Americans

COMMON NORWEGIAN NOUNS

Below is a list of common Norwegian nouns. The plural form is given in parentheses. Note that some nouns do not have a plural form in Norwegian.

ANIMALS

et dyr (dyr) – an animal (animals)
en hund (hunder) – a dog (dogs)
en katt (katter) – a cat (cats)
en fisk (fisker) – a fish (fish)
en fugl (fugle) – a bird (birds)
en ku (kuer) – a cow (cows)
et svin (svin) – a pig (pig)
en mus (mus) – a mouse (mice)
en hest (hester) – a horse (horses)

PEOPLE

en person (personer) – a person (people)
en mor (mødre) – a mother (mothers)
en far (fedre) – a father (fathers)
en sønn (sønner) – a son (sons)
en datter (døtre) – a daughter (daughters)
en bror (brødre) – a brother (brothers)
en søster (søstre) – a sister (sisters)
en mann (menn) – a man (men)
en kvinne (kvinner) – a woman (women)
en gutt (gutter) – a boy (boys)
en jente (jenter) – a girl (girls)
et barn (barn) – a child (children)
en venn (venner) – a friend (friends)

PARTS OF THE BODY

en krop (kropper) – a body (bodies)
et hode (hoder) – a head (heads)
et ansikt (ansikter) – a face (faces)
et hår (hår) – a hair (hairs)
et øye (øyne) – an eye (eyes)
en munn (munner) – a mouth (mouths)
en nese (neser) – a nose (noses)
et øre (ører) – an ear (ears)
en hånd (hender) – a hand (hands)
en arm (arme) – an arm (arms)
en fot (føtter) – a foot (feet)
et ben (ben) – a leg (legs)
et hjerte (hjerter) – a heart (hearts)
et blod – blood
et bein (bein) – a bone (bones)
et skjegg (skjegg) – a beard (beards)

FOOD & DRINK

en mat – food
et kjøtt – meat
et brød (brød) – bread (breads)
en ost (oster) – cheese (cheeses)
et eple (epler) – apple (apples)
et vann – water
et øl (øl) – beer
en vin (viner) – wine (wines)
en kaffe – coffee
en te – tea
en melk – milk

PRONOUNS

Norwegian pronouns are very similar to English. The subject pronouns are:

jeg – I (**jeg** rhymes with "die").
du – you
De – you (polite form)
han – he
hun – she
den / det – it
vi – we
dere – you (plural)
de – they (**de** is pronounced "dee")

Note that there are two forms for "it"; **den** is used for masculine and feminine nouns and **det** for neuter nouns. Also note that Norwegian has a polite form of "you" and a plural form of "you" used when speaking to more than one person. Standard English does not have this plural form but some regional forms exist, such as "y'all".

Just like in English, Norwegian has a different set of object pronouns (the difference between "I" and "me" in English). The object pronouns are:

meg – me (**meg** sounds like "my")
deg – you (**deg** sounds like "die")
Dem – you (polite form)
ham – him
henne – her
den / det – it
oss – us
dere – you (plural)
dem – them

Jeg elsker deg
I love you

Du elsker meg
You love me

Han elsker henne
He loves her

Hun elsker ham
She loves him

Norwegian also has a set of possessive pronouns that correspond to the English "my", "your" etc. The possessive pronouns are:

min / mi / mitt / mine – my / mine
din / di / ditt / dine – your / yours
Deres – your / yours (polite form)
hans – his
hennes – her
dens / dets – its
vår / vår / vårt / våre – our / ours
deres – your (plural) / yours (plural)
deres – their / theirs

The forms for "my", "your" and "our" change form depending on the gender of the noun that is owned.

min arm
my arm

mi nese / min nese
my nose

mitt hår
my hair

dine hester
your horses

The masculine possessive form can be used for feminine nouns and is not considered wrong.

The possessive pronouns in Norwegian are used for both the possessive pronouns and the possessive adjectives, meaning that the same word is used for the English "my" and "mine".

min hund
my dog

hunden er min
the dog is mine

NORWEGIAN VERBS:
PRESENT AND PAST TENSES

PRESENT TENSE

This is where Norwegian gets easy!

Conjugating verbs is one way where Norwegian is simpler than most European languages including English. In Norwegian, verbs do not change form for person or number, meaning that in any given tense there is only a single form of the verb and there are no exceptions.

To illustrate this let's look at three verbs: "to be", "to have" and "to love". Notice that there are various different forms in English, but there is only a single form in Norwegian:

jeg er – I am
du er – you are
hun er – she is
vi er – we are
dere er – you (plural) are
de er – they are

jeg har – I have
du har – you have
hun har – she has
vi har – we have
dere har – you (plural) have
de har – they have

jeg elsker – I love
du elsker – you love
han elsker – he loves
vi elsker – we love
dere elsker – you (plural) love
de elsker – they love

As you can see this is simpler than English and much simpler than languages like Spanish and Italian that have a different form for each person.

To negate verbs you simply add **ikke** after the verb that you want to negate:

han elsker ikke
he does not love

PAST TENSE

Just like English, Norwegian verbs have two different past tense forms, called "weak verbs" and "strong verbs". The weak verbs, also called "regular verbs", in English are verbs that simply add a – d or –ed ending to form the past tense, such as walk – walked, admire – admired, escape – escaped etc.

The most common type of weak verb in Norwegian adds –et to the basic form of the verb to make the past tense. As in the present tense, the same form of the verb is used regardless of person.

jeg arbeider – **jeg arbeidet**
I work – I worked

du lager – **du laget**
you cook – you cooked

Some weak verbs in Norwegian add –te to the stem of the verb instead of –et to form the past tense.

vi spiser – vi spiste
we eat – we ate

de leker – de lekte
they play – they played

A few Norwegian weak verbs add –**dde** to the stem of the verb.

jeg bor – jeg bodde
I live (reside) – I lived (resided)

Norwegian strong verbs involve a vowel change to the stem in order to form the past tense. This corresponds to English irregular verbs such as drink – drank, run – ran, fly – flew. Like in English the strong verbs in Norwegian are irregular and there is no general rule that can be learned as a shortcut. The number of Norwegian strong verbs is relatively small, but many are high frequency words that are used all the time. Many verbs that are irregular in English are also irregular in Norwegian, such as:

jeg gir dig
I give you

du gav mig
you gave me

hun gå
she goes

han gikk
he went

COMMON NORWEGIAN VERBS

Below is a list of common verbs in Norwegian, listed with the infinitive, the present tense form and the past tense form. Note that many common verbs are similar to English.

være – **er** – **var** – to be
ha – **har** – **hadde** – to have
gjøre – **gjør** – **gjorde** – to do
si – **sier** – **sa** – to say
snakke – **snakker** – **snakket** – to speak
se – **ser** – **så** – to see
gå – **går** – **gikk** – to go / to walk
løpe – **løper** – **løp** – to run
hoppe – **hopper** – **hoppet** – to jump
arbeide – **arbeider** – **arbeidet** – to work
leke – **leker** – **lekte** – to play
fly – **flyer** – **fløy** – to fly
svømme – **svømmer** – **svømte** – to swim
spise – **spiser** – **spiste** – to eat
drikke – **drikker** – **drak** – to drink
lage – **lager** – **laget** – to cook
le – **ler** – **lo** – to laugh
gråte – **gråter** – **gråt** – to cry
sitte – **sitter** – **sat** – to sit
stå – **står** – **stod** – to stand
elske – **esker** – **elsket** – to love
like – **liker** – **likte** – to like
hate – **hater** – **hatet** – to hate
kysse – **kysser** – **kysset** – to kiss
danse – **danser** – **danset** – to dance
sove – **sover** – **sov** – to sleep
synge – **synger** – **sang** – to sing
lære – **lærer** – **lærte** – to learn / to teach

29

tenke – tenker – tenkte – to think
lese – leser – leste – to read
skrive – skriver – skrev – to write
åpne – åpner – åpnet – to open
lukke – lukker – lukket – to close
kjøpe – kjøper – kjøpte – to buy
betale – betaler – betalte – to pay
selge – selger – solgte – to sell

ADJECTIVES

Adjectives in Norwegian inflect for gender and number.

As we have already seen, when you want to say "the dog" or "the house", the definite article is added to the end of the word.

hunden
the dog

huset
the house

husene
the houses

If you want to add an adjective to this phrase and say "the big dog", a different form of "the" is also added before the adjective. This form depends on the gender and number of the noun, **den** for masculine and feminine, **det** for neuter and **de** for plural.

den store hunden
the big dog

det store huset
the big house

de store husene
the big houses

The word for "big" in Norwegian is **stor**, however between "the" and the noun an –e is added in each case to make **store**. If instead you want to say "a big dog", in Norwegian it is a little more complicated. In this case there are three forms of the adjective

31

depending again on the gender and number of the noun. The three forms are as follows:

en stor hund
a big dog

et stort hus
a big house

store hus
big houses

The three forms of the adjective are: no ending for masculine and feminine nouns, **–t** for neuter nouns and **–e** for plural nouns. The same three forms are used if instead of "a big dog" you want to say "the dog is big".

hunden er stor
the dog is big

huset er stort
the house is big

husene er store
the houses are big

This is the basic pattern in Norwegian for all adjectives; however there are a few exceptions that have to be learned on a case by case basis.

NORWEGIAN NUMBERS, DAYS AND MONTHS

NUMBERS

en – one
to – two
tre – three
fire – four
fem – five
seks – six
sju – seven
åtte – eight
ni – nine
ti – ten
elleve – eleven
tolv – twelve
tretten – thirteen
fjorten – fourteen
femten – fifteen
seksten – sixteen
sytten – seventeen
atten – eighteen
nitten – nineteen
tyve – twenty
tretti – thirty
førti – forty
femti – fifty
seksti – sixty
sytti – seventy
åtti – eighty
nitti – ninety
ett hundre – one hundred

DAYS OF THE WEEK

mandag – Monday
tirsdag – Tuesday
onsdag – Wednesday
torsdag – Thursday
fredag – Friday
lørdag – Saturday
søndag – Sunday

MONTHS OF THE YEAR

januar – January
februar – February
mars – March
april – April
mai – May
juni – June
juli – July
august – August
september – September
oktober – October
november – November
desember – December

USEFUL NORWEGIAN PHRASES

Hei
Hi

Hvordan har du det?
How are you?

Bare bra, takk.
Just fine, thank you

Ja
Yes

Nei
No

Hva heter du?
What is your name?

Jeg heter Anne.
My name is Anne.

Hyggelig å møte deg.
Nice to meet you.

Hvor er du fra?
Where are you from?

Jeg kommer fra Norge.
I am from Norway

God morgen
Good morning

God ettermiddag
Good afternoon

God kveld
Good evening

God natt
Good night

Ha det bra
Good bye

Unnskyld
Excuse me

Vær så snill
Please

Takk
Thank you

Jeg forstår ikke
I don't understand

Jeg vet ikke
I don't know

Snakker du engelsk?
Do you speak English?

Snakker De norsk?
Do you speak Norwegian?

Ja, litt.
Yes, a little.

Jeg snakker ikke godt norsk
I don't speak Norwegian well

GLOSSARY – THEMATIC ORDER

ANIMALS

dyr (–et, –)	animal
hund (–en, –er)	dog
katt (–en, –er)	cat
fisk (–en, –er)	fish
fugl (–en, –er)	bird
ku (–a or –en, –er)	cow
svin (–et, –)	pig
mus (–a or –en, –)	mouse
hest (–en, –er)	horse

PEOPLE

person (–en, –er)	person
mor (–a or –en, mødre)	mother
far (–en, fedre)	father
sønn (–en, –er)	son
datter (–a or –en, døtre)	daughter
bror (–en, brødre)	brother
søster (–a or –en, søstre)	sister
venn (–en, –er)	friend
mann (–en, menn)	man
kvinne (–a or –en, –r)	woman
gutt (–en, –er)	boy
jente (–a or –en, –r)	girl
barn (–et, –)	child

LOCATION

by (–en, –er)	city
hus (–et, hus)	house
gate (–a or –en, –r)	street
flyplass (–en, –er)	airport
hotell (–et, –er)	hotel
restaurant (–en, –er)	restaurant
skole (–n, –r)	school
universitet (–et, –er)	university
park (–en, –er)	park
butikk (–en, –er)	store / shop
sykehus (–et, –)	hospital
kirke (–a or –en, –r)	church
land (–et, –)	country (state)
bank (–en, –er)	bank
marked (–et, –er)	market

HOME

bord (–et, –er)	table
stol (–en, –er)	chair
vindu (–et, –er)	window
dør (–a or –en, –er)	door
bok (–a or –en, bøker)	book

CLOTHING

klesplagg (–et, –)	clothing
hatt (–en, –er)	hat
kjole (–n, –r)	dress
skjorte (–a or –en, –r)	shirt
bukse (–n, –r)	pants
sko (–en, –)	shoe

BODY

kropp (–en, –er)	body
hode (–t, –r)	head
ansikt (–et, –er)	face
hår (–et, –)	hair
øye (–t, øyne)	eye
munn (–en, –er)	mouth
nese (–a or –en, –r)	nose
øre (–t, –r)	ear
hånd (–a or –en, hender)	hand
arm (–en, –er)	arm
fot (–en, føtter)	foot
ben (–et, –)	leg
hjerte (–t, –r)	heart
blod (–et)	blood
bein (–et, –)	bone
skjegg (–et, –)	beard

MISCELLANEOUS

ja	yes
nei	no

FOOD & DRINK

mat (–en)	food
kjøtt (–et)	meat
brød (–et, –)	bread
ost (–en, –er)	cheese
eple (–et, –er)	apple
vann (–et, –)	water
øl (–let, –)	beer
vin (–en, –er)	wine
kaffe (–n)	coffee
te (–en)	tea
melk (–a or –en)	milk

frokost (–en, –er)	breakfast
lunsj (–en, –er)	lunch
middag (–en, –er)	dinner

COLORS

farge (–n, –r)	color
rød (–t, –e)	red
blå (–tt, –)	blue
grønn (grønt, –e)	green
gul (–t, –e)	yellow
svart (–, –e)	black
hvit (–t, –e)	white

NATURE

hav (–et, –)	sea
elv (–a or –en, –er)	river
innsjø (–en, –er)	lake
fjell (–et, –)	mountain
regn (–et)	rain
snø (–en)	snow
tre (–et, trær)	tree
blomst (–en, –er)	flower
sol (–a or –en, –er)	sun
måne (–n, –r)	moon
vind (–en, –er)	wind
himmel (–en, himler)	sky
ild (–en)	fire
is (–en, –er)	ice

COMMON VERBS

være (er, var)	be
ha (har, hadde)	have
gjøre (gjør, gjorde)	do
si (–er, sa)	say
snakke (–r, –et)	speak
se (–r, så)	see
gå (–r, gikk)	go / walk
løpe (–r, løp)	run
hoppe (–r, –et)	jump
arbeide (–r, –et)	work
leke (–r, lekte)	play
fly (–r, fløy)	fly
svømme (–r, svømte)	swim
spise (–r, spiste)	eat
drikke (–r, drak)	drink
lage (–r, –et)	cook
le (–r, lo)	laugh
gråte (–r, gråt)	cry
sitte (–r, satt)	sit
stå (–r, stod)	stand
elske (–r, –et)	love
like (–r, likte)	like
hate (–r, –t)	hate
kysse (–r, –et)	kiss
danse (–r, –et)	dance
sove (–r, sov)	sleep
synge (–r, sang)	sing
lære (–r, lærte)	learn
tenke (–r, tenkte)	think
lese (–r, leste)	read
skrive (–r, skrev)	write
åpne (–r, –et)	open
lukke (–r, –et)	close
kjøpe (–r, kjøpte)	buy
betale (–r, betalte)	pay
selge (–r, solgte)	sell

ADJECTIVES

stor (–t, –e)	big
liten (lite, små)	small
god (–t, –e)	good
dårlig(– , –e)	bad
varm (–t, –e)	hot
kald (–t, –e)	cold
billig (–, –e)	cheap
dyr (–t, –e)	expensive
glad (–, –e)	happy
trist (trist, –e)	sad

TIME

dag (–en, –er)	day
måned (–en, –er)	month
år (–et, –)	year
time (–n, –r)	hour
i dag	today
i morgen	tomorrow
i går	yesterday

SEASONS

sommer (–en, somre)	summer
høst (–en, –er)	fall
vinter (–en, vintre)	winter
vår (–en, –er)	spring

GLOSSARY – ALPHABETICAL ORDER

A

ansikt (–et, –er)	face
april	April
arbeide (–r, –et)	work
arm (–en, –er)	arm
atten	eighteen
august	August

B

bank (–en, –er)	bank
barn (–et, –)	child
bein (–et, –)	bone
ben (–et, –)	leg
betale (–r, betalte)	pay
billig (–, –e)	cheap
blod (–et)	blood
blomst (–en, –er)	flower
blå (–tt, –)	blue
bok (–a or –en, bøker)	book
bord (–et, –er)	table
bror (–en, brødre)	brother
brød (–et, –)	bread
bukse (–n, –r)	pants
butikk (–en, –er)	store / shop
by (–en, –er)	city

D

dag (–en, –er)	day
danse (–r, –et)	dance
datter (–a or –en, døtre)	daughter
desember	December
drikke (–r, drak)	drink
dyr (–et, –)	animal
dyr (–t, –e)	expensive
dør (–a or –en, –er)	door
dårlig(– , –e)	bad

E

elleve	eleven
elske (–r, –et)	love
elv (–a or –en, –er)	river
en	one
eple (–et, –er)	apple

F

far (–en, fedre)	father
farge (–n, –r)	color
februar	February
fem	five
femten	fifteen
femti	fifty
fire	four
fisk (–en, –er)	fish
fjell (–et, –)	mountain
fjorten	fourteen
fly (–r, fløy)	fly
flyplass (–en, –er)	airport
fot (–en, føtter)	foot
fredag	Friday
frokost (–en, –er)	breakfast

fugl (–en, –er)	bird
førti	forty

G

gate (–a or –en, –r)	street
gjøre (gjør, gjorde)	do
glad (–, –e)	happy
god (–t, –e)	good
grønn (grønt, –e)	green
gråte (–r, gråt)	cry
gul (–t, –e)	yellow
gutt (–en, –er)	boy
gå (–r, gikk)	go / walk

H

hate (–r, –t)	hate
hatt (–en, –er)	hat
hav (–et, –)	sea
hest (–en, –er)	horse
himmel (–en, himler)	sky
hjerte (–t, –r)	heart
hode (–t, –r)	head
hoppe (–r, –et)	jump
hotell (–et, –er)	hotel
hund (–en, –er)	dog
hundre	hundred
hus (–et, hus)	house
hvit (–t, –e)	white
høst (–en, –er)	fall
hånd (–a or –en, hender)	hand
hår (–et, –)	hair

I

i dag	today
i går	yesterday
i morgen	tomorrow
ild (–en)	fire
innsjø (–en, –er)	lake
is (–en, –er)	ice

J

ja	yes
januar	January
jente (–a or –en, –r)	girl
juli	July
juni	June

K

kaffe (–n)	coffee
kald (–t, –e)	cold
katt (–en, –er)	cat
kirke (–a or –en, –r)	church
kjole (–n, –r)	dress
kjøpe (–r, kjøpte)	buy
kjøtt (–et)	meat
klesplagg (–et, –)	clothing
kropp (–en, –er)	body
ku (–a or –en, –er)	cow
kvinne (–a or –en, –r)	woman
kysse (–r, –et)	kiss

L

lage (–r, –et)	cook
land (–et, –)	country (state)
le (–r, lo)	laugh
leke (–r, lekte)	play
lese (–r, leste)	read
like (–r, likte)	like
liten (lite, små)	small
lukke (–r, –et)	close
lunsj (–en, –er)	lunch
lære (–r, lærte)	learn
løpe (–r, løp)	run
lørdag	Saturday

M

mai	May
mandag	Monday
mann (–en, menn)	man
marked (–et, –er)	market
mars	March
mat (–en)	food
melk (–a or –en)	milk
middag (–en, –er)	dinner
mor (–a or –en, mødre)	mother
munn (–en, –er)	mouth
mus (–a or –en, –)	mouse
måne (–n, –r)	moon
måned (–en, –er)	month

N

nei	no
nese (–a or –en, –r)	nose
ni	nine
nitten	nineteen

nitti	ninety
november	November

O

oktober	October
onsdag	Wednesday
ost (–en, –er)	cheese

P

park (–en, –er)	park
person (–en, –er)	person

R

regn (–et)	rain
restaurant (–en, –er)	restaurant
rød (–t, –e)	red

S

se (–r, så)	see
seks	six
seksten	sixteen
seksti	sixty
selge (–r, solgte)	sell
september	September
si (–er, sa)	say
sitte (–r, satt)	sit
sju	seven
skjegg (–et, –)	beard
skjorte (–a or –en, –r)	shirt
sko (–en, –)	shoe

skole (–n, –r)	school
skrive (–r, skrev)	write
snakke (–r, –et)	speak
snø (–en)	snow
sol (–a or –en, –er)	sun
sommer (–en, somre)	summer
sove (–r, sov)	sleep
spise (–r, spiste)	eat
stol (–en, –er)	chair
stor (–t, –e)	big
stå (–r, stod)	stand
svart (–, –e)	black
svin (–et, –)	pig
svømme (–r, svømte)	swim
sykehus (–et, –)	hospital
synge (–r, sang)	sing
sytten	seventeen
sytti	seventy
søndag	Sunday
sønn (–en, –er)	son
søster (–a or –en, søstre)	sister

T

te (–en)	tea
tenke (–r, tenkte)	think
ti	ten
time (–n, –r)	hour
tirsdag	Tuesday
to	two
tolv	twelve
torsdag	Thursday
tre	three
tre (–et, trær)	tree
tretten	thirteen
tretti	thirty
trist (trist, –e)	sad
tusen	thousand
tyve	twenty

U

universitet (–et, –er)   university

V

vann (–et, –)	water
vår (–en, –er)	spring
varm (–t, –e)	hot
venn (–en, –er)	friend
vin (–en, –er)	wine
vind (–en, –er)	wind
vindu (–et, –er)	window
vinter (–en, vintre)	winter
være (er, var)	be

Ø

øl (–let, –)	beer
øre (–t, –r)	ear
øye (–t, øyne)	eye

Å

åpne (–r, –t)	open
år (–et, –)	year
åtte	eight
åtti	eighty

CPSIA information can be obtained
at www.ICGtesting.com
Printed in the USA
LVHW080823271121
704609LV00040B/3913

9 780995 930520